CW00864398

# GOING TO THE MOON

by Mae and Ira Freeman
illustrated by Lee Ames

COLLINS AND HARVILL

Trademark of Random House, Inc., William Collins Sons & Co. Ltd., Authorised User

ISBN 0 00 171147 4

Copyright © 1959, 1971 by Mae Freeman and Ira Freeman

A Beginner Book published by arrangement with Random House Inc., New York, New York

First published in Great Britain 1973

Printed in Great Britain
Collins Clear-Type Press: London and Glasgow

# GOING TO THE MOON

The moon is up there, far away.
Would you like to go there?
Some day you may.

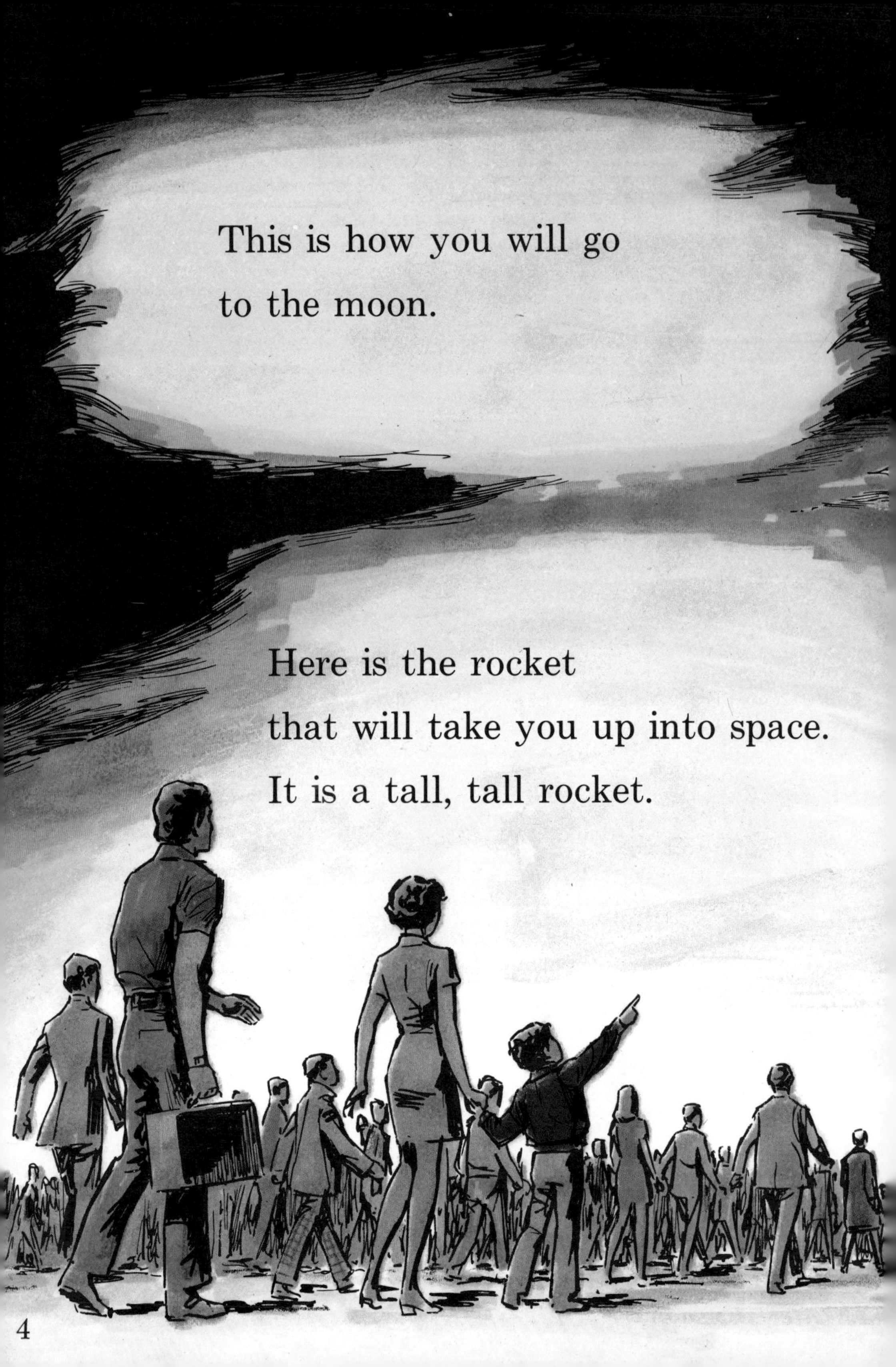

This is how you will go
to the moon.

Here is the rocket
that will take you up into space.
It is a tall, tall rocket.

A tall tower stands next to
the rocket.
There is a car inside the tower.
The astronauts go into the car
with you.

Now you ride all the way up
to the top.

Come on in.

Come into the rocket.

This is where you will sit.
You will sit here
with the astronauts.

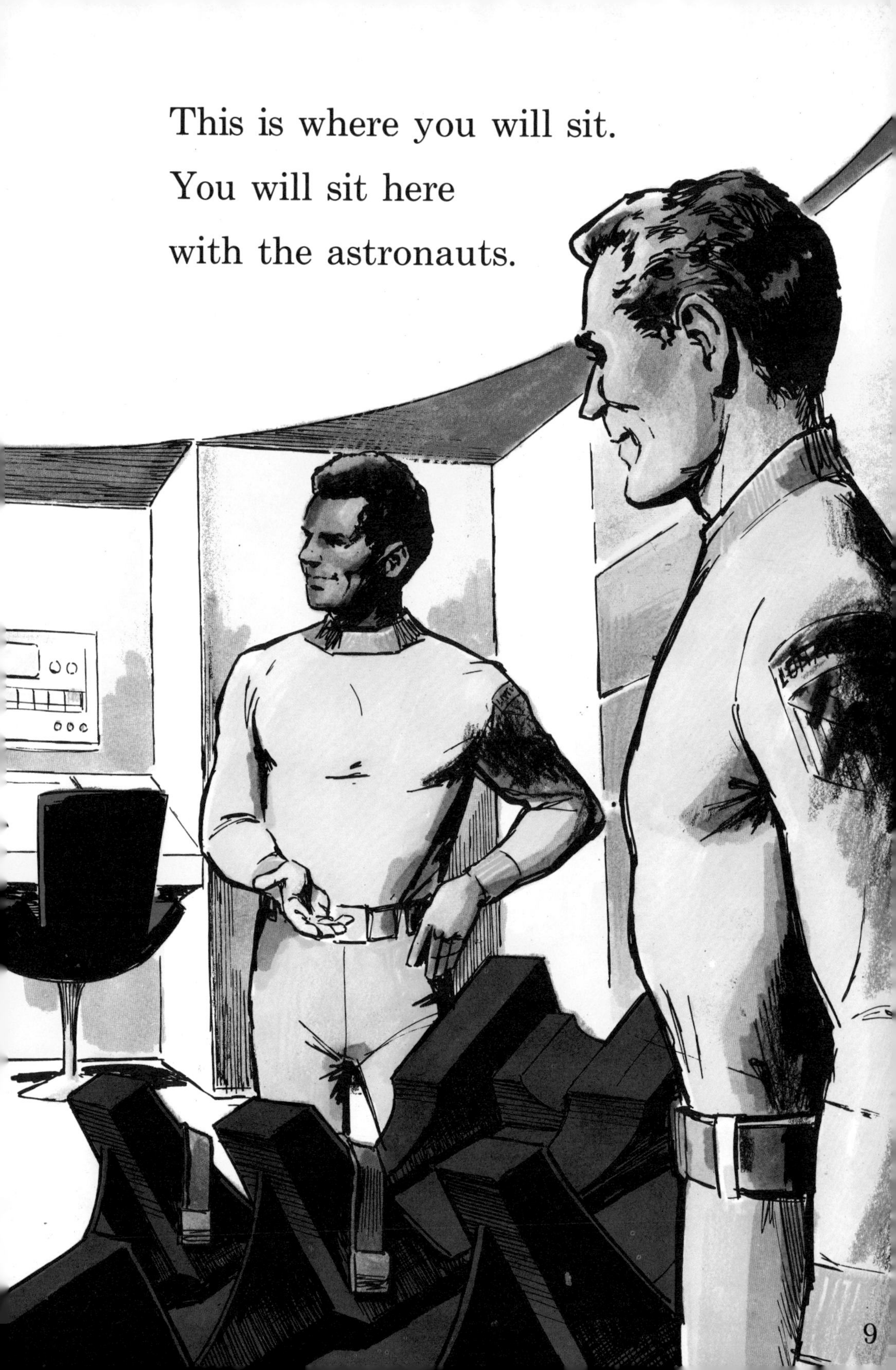

The astronauts will show you
what to do.

Hook on that belt.
Hook it on tight.
Get set to go!

VROOOM!

At last!

The rocket is off!

And you are in it!

You feel the rocket shake.

You feel the push . . . PUSH . . . P U S H !

But you do not fall off your seat.

The strong push holds you in tight.

Your rocket keeps going
faster and faster.
You are out in space now.
Turn your head a little.
Then you can look out the window.
Can you guess what you will see?

You see the sky . . .

and it is not blue any more.

The sky looks black!

The sky always looks black

out here in space.

What is that bright spot
out there so far away?
It is the space station.
Your rocket is going there.
BUT . . .

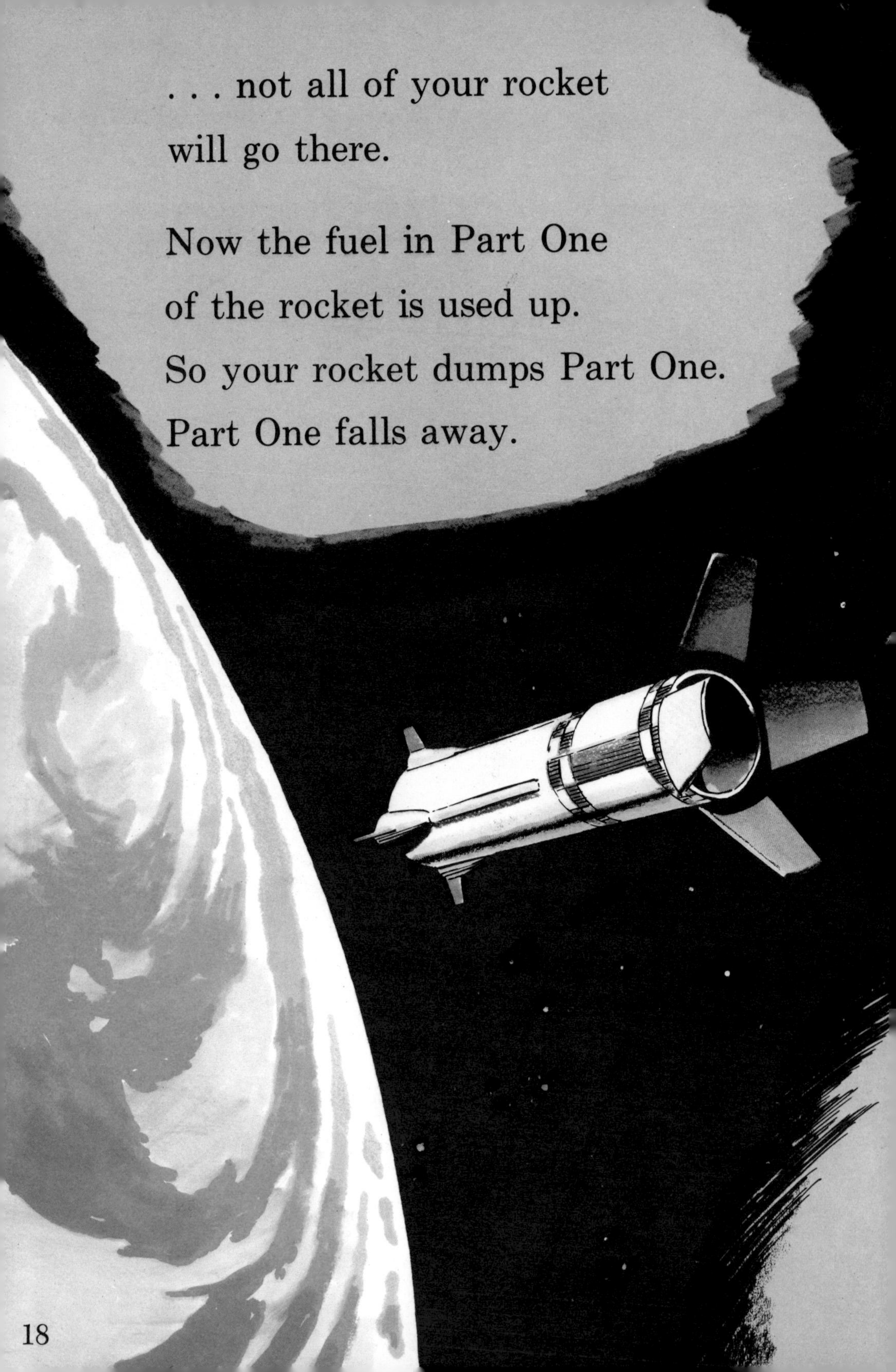

. . . not all of your rocket
will go there.

Now the fuel in Part One
of the rocket is used up.
So your rocket dumps Part One.
Part One falls away.

Now there is only Part Two
of the rocket.
AND YOU ARE IN IT!

Part Two fires!
On and on you go,
out into space.

Open your belt.
OH! Up you float,
off your seat!
You cannot stay down.
You float because
YOU ARE A SPACE MAN NOW!

At home all things stay down.
The pull of the earth
holds them down.
This pull is called gravity.
But gravity cannot hold
you down out here
in space.

Soon you are near the space station.
It does not look like a little spot
any more.
Now you can see that the
space station is a huge ring.
And you can see the ring turning.
It keeps turning all the time.

You will stop at the space station
on the way to the moon.
Get ready to dock!

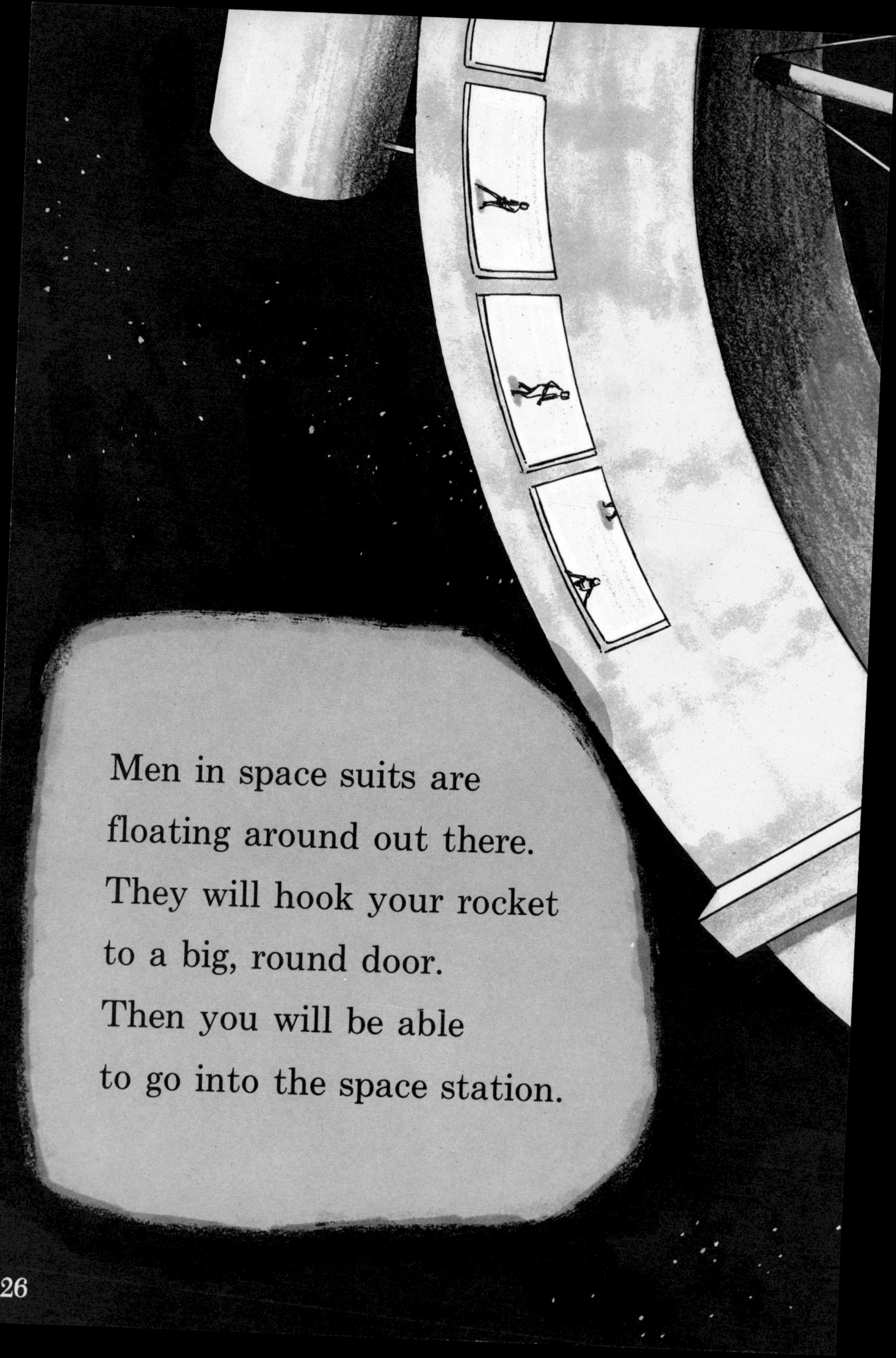

Men in space suits are
floating around out there.
They will hook your rocket
to a big, round door.
Then you will be able
to go into the space station.

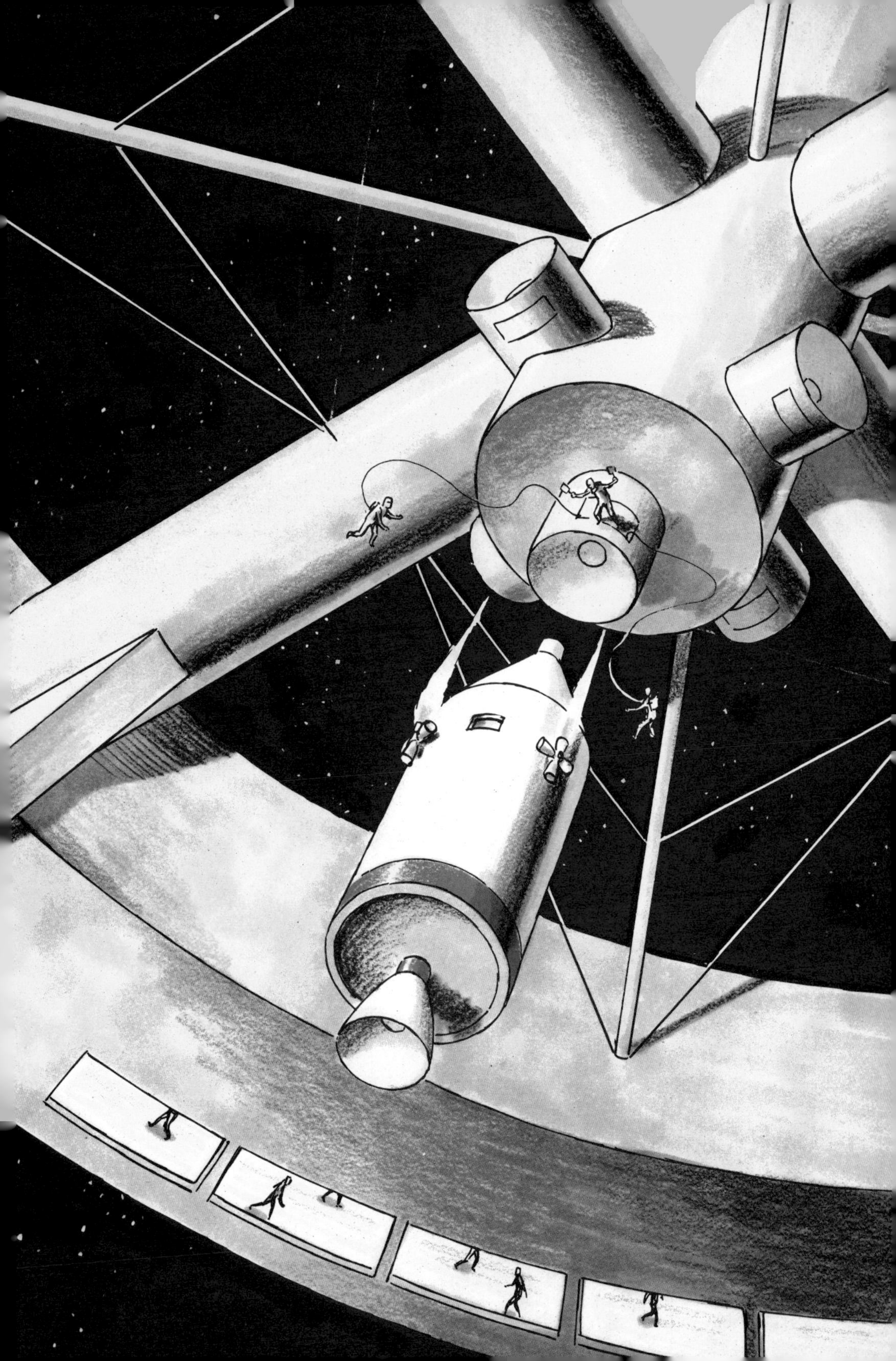

Come into the space station.
Here things stay down again.
You will stay down, too.
Why?
The space station is turning
all the time.
This makes things stay down.
It is just like having
gravity again.

There are things to do here.
You can watch TV.
There are good things to eat.
You may take pictures
to show to your friends
back home.

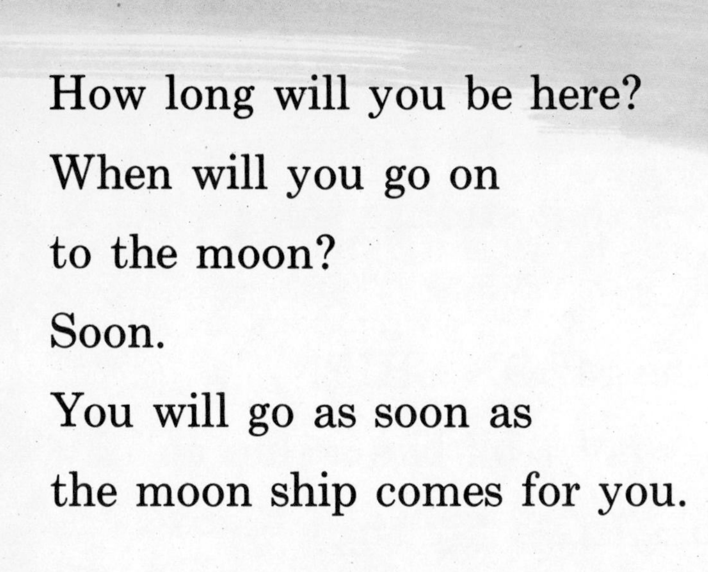

How long will you be here?

When will you go on

to the moon?

Soon.

You will go as soon as

the moon ship comes for you.

Look out the window.
What is that strange thing
out there?
It is the MOON SHIP!
It does not look like a ship at all.
It looks like a big bug
with bent legs.

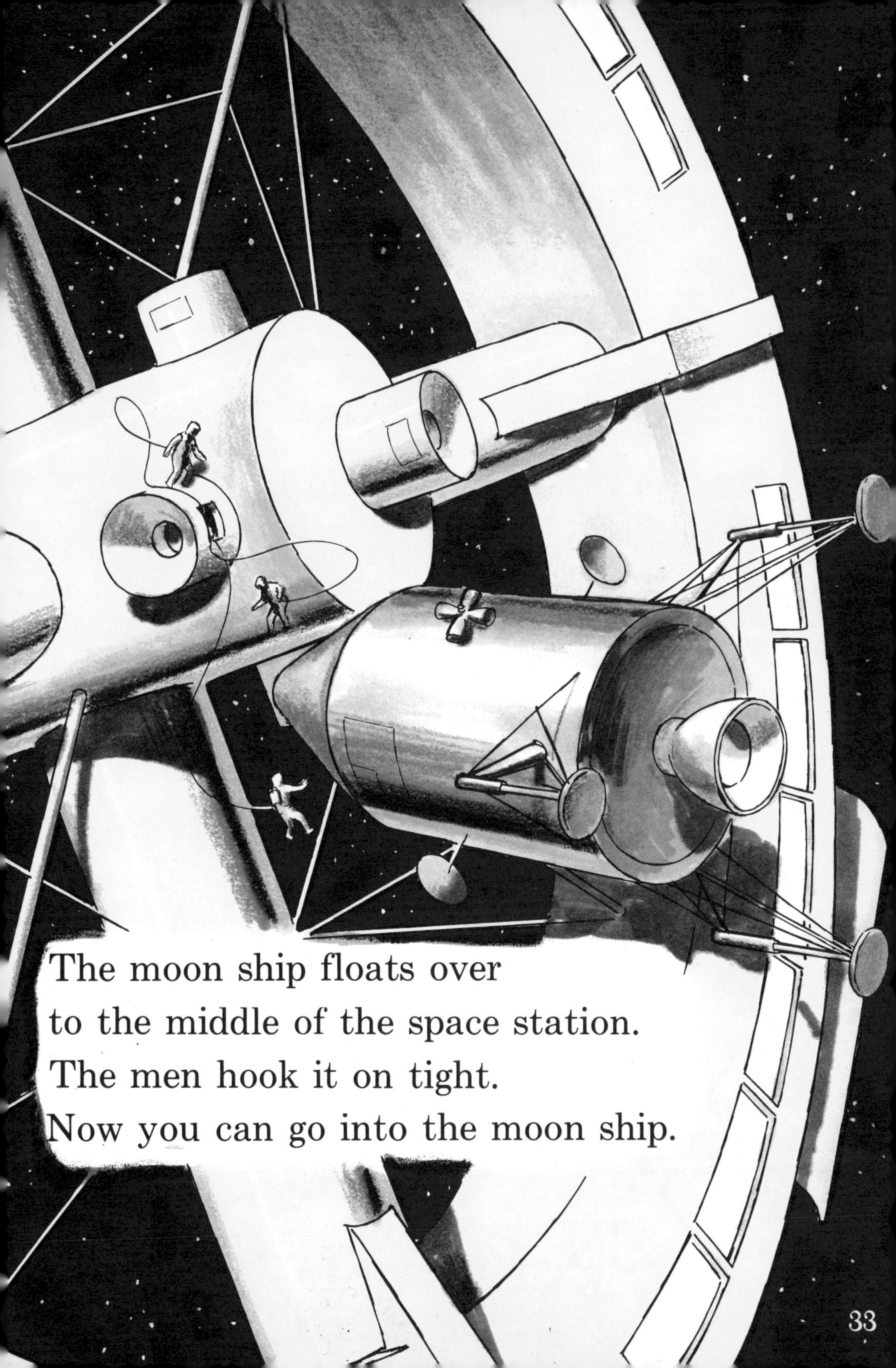

The moon ship floats over
to the middle of the space station.
The men hook it on tight.
Now you can go into the moon ship.

The moon ship is not like
the space station.
Things do not stay down
in the moon ship.

Give yourself a little push.
You can float right to your seat!

There is a rocket at the bottom
of the moon ship.
The rocket fires.
You feel the big push.
Your ship gets away fast.
THEN . . .

THE ROCKETS STOP!

They gave the moon ship
a big push.
That is all it needs.
Now your ship will go on and on
by itself.

There is nothing to hold
the ship back.
It doesn't even have to push
through air.
There is no air at all
out in space.

You will be in the moon ship
for three days.
That is how long it takes
to get to the moon.
There are books and games
and TV, too.
There are many things you can do
to help the astronauts.
How fast the three days go!

At last!

This is the big day.

The moon is very near now.

It looks like a huge ball.

It has holes and bumps all over it.

How will your moon ship land?

The astronauts fire a little side rocket.

It makes the ship turn.

Now it can land on its legs.

Get set to land on the moon!

Now the bottom rocket
fires again.
It fires straight down.
This lets the moon ship
come down slowly.
It lands on its long legs
without a bump.

YOU ARE ON THE MOON!
But you cannot go out yet.
There is no air out there
for you to breathe.
You could not live
in the hot, hot days on the moon.
You could not live
in the cold, cold nights on the moon.
So you must wear a special space suit.
There is a radio in it.
That is how you and the astronauts
can talk to each other.

Now you are ready
to walk on the moon!

The moon does not look
like the earth at all.
There are no trees!
No lakes or rivers!
No water at all!
The ground looks like sand.

There is a big hole over there.
It looks like a giant soup bowl.
This is called a crater.
There are many, many craters
all over the moon.

Look over there! What do you see?
Here comes a moon car!
It will take you for a ride.

Away you go in the moon car.
You come to a big crater.
But this does not stop your moon car.
It goes right down into the crater.
Down . . . down.

Then up . . . up. And out.

The car stops near a hill.

You can get out and have some fun.

Look what you can do!
You can get to that hill
in five big steps.

You can see more
from the top of the hill.
Do you see that house over there?
That is the moon house.
That is where you will stay
until you go back home.

It is easy to get to the moon house.

Come inside.

Now you can take off your space suit.

People work here to find out
more about the moon.
And more about things in space.
Some of them watch the stars
through a big telescope.

Look up at the sky.
Do you see that big dot
shining out there?
That is Mars.
Mars is a long, long way
from the moon.

What would you find on Mars?
No one has been there yet.
But some day YOU may go there.
Then you will see.